D1620019

THIS BOOK BELONGS TO:

_____

_____

_____

The animals from the forest live in a magical world where they all get along and work together.

Once upon a time, in a beautiful forest, there lived a variety of animals. There were rabbits, squirrels, deer, and even a family of bears. The animals all lived in harmony and enjoyed spending their days playing and exploring the forest.

One day, a group of mischievous monkeys came to the forest. They were loud and boisterous, and they loved to cause trouble. They would swing from tree to tree, making a mess wherever they went.

The other animals were not happy with the monkeys' behavior and tried to ignore them. But the monkeys just kept causing more and more problems.

One day, a wise old owl had an idea. He flew to the top of a tall tree and called all the animals to come and listen.

"We must do something about the monkeys," the owl said. "They are ruining our beautiful forest with their mischief and mayhem."

The animals all nodded in agreement. They knew the owl was right.

"We could try talking to them," suggested a friendly rabbit. "Maybe if we explain how their actions are affecting the forest and all of us, they will change their ways."

The other animals thought this was a good idea, so they went to the monkeys and had a heart-to-heart talk. The monkeys listened carefully and realized that their behavior was not only causing problems for the other animals, but also for themselves. They promised to be more mindful of their actions and to respect the forest and its inhabitants.

The end.

Thanke you

We hope you enjoyed our book

As a small family company,your

feedback is very important to us.

Please let us know how you like our

book at:

deeasybooks@yahoo.com

 facebook.com/deeasybooks

 instagram.com/deeasybooks/

CPSIA information can be obtained
at www.ICGtesting.com
Printed in the USA
BVHW020238210123
656715BV00011B/453